汪汪游行庆典

Happy Halloween

[美]威力·布莱文斯/著　[美]吉姆·帕约/绘

王婧/译

电子工业出版社.

Publishing House of Electronics Industry

北京·BEIJING

Ick and Crud. Book 6, Happy Halloween / by Wiley Blevins; illustrated by Jim Paillot.

版权贸易合同登记号　图字：01-2022-0735

图书在版编目（CIP）数据

汪汪游行庆典 / (美) 威力·布莱文斯 (Wiley Blevins) 著；(美) 吉姆·帕约 (Jim Paillot) 绘；王婧
译. -- 北京：电子工业出版社，2023.6
（胖狗和瘦狗）
ISBN 978-7-121-44941-3

Ⅰ.①汪… Ⅱ.①威… ②吉… ③王… Ⅲ.①儿童故事－图画故事－美国－现代 Ⅳ.①I712.85

中国国家版本馆CIP数据核字(2023)第077357号

责任编辑：范丽鹏
印　　刷：天津图文方嘉印刷有限公司
装　　订：天津图文方嘉印刷有限公司
出版发行：电子工业出版社
　　　　　北京市海淀区万寿路 173 信箱　邮编：100036
开　　本：787×1092　1/16　印张：26.25　字数：264 千字
版　　次：2023 年 6 月第 1 版
印　　次：2023 年 6 月第 1 次印刷
定　　价：208.00 元 (全 8 册)

凡所购买电子工业出版社图书有缺损问题，请向购买书店调换。若书店售缺，请与本社发行
部联系，联系及邮购电话：(010) 88254888，88258888。
质量投诉请发邮件至 zlts@phei.com.cn，盗版侵权举报请发邮件至 dbqq@phei.com.cn。
本书咨询联系方式：(010) 88254161 转 1862，fanlp@phei.com.cn。

目 录

闪亮登场的主角们

艾克

克鲁德

绒球小姐

鲍勃

马丁太太

"嘣！"克鲁德突然大叫一声。

"哇！啊！哇！你吓得我差点灵魂出窍了！"艾克大叫。

"已经到了每年的那个时候啦！"克鲁德说。

"你是说坏牙的南瓜、女巫，还有装扮成幽灵的孩子们，是吗？"艾克问。

"是的！"克鲁德兴奋地说，"要过节啦！"

　　艾克吓得浑身发抖："这个时候会有很多很多的幽灵，我害怕幽灵，而且他们住在阁楼里，他们还会吃小狗狗。"

　　"我会保护你的，哥们儿。"克鲁德说。

　　这时，鲍勃抱着两个盒子走了进来，每个盒子上面都写着："狗狗服装"。

"哦吼。"艾克说。

"今年想都别想，"克鲁德说，"他休想再把我打扮成一根热狗了。"

"你这已经算是不错了，"艾克抱怨道，"鲍勃去年把我放到婴儿车里，我还要拿着婴儿摇铃。孩子们看到我的样子时，吓得尖叫着就昏倒了。"

"好吧，所以今年我们一定不能再让事情重演了。"克鲁德说道，"跟紧我。"

"我已经像泡泡糖似的黏着你了。"艾克说。

3

　　"快过来啊，克鲁德！"鲍勃叫道。克鲁德就像没听见似的。"克鲁德，"鲍勃又叫道，"快过来呀！"

　　"我才不去呢。"克鲁德小声嘟囔。

　　"我也不去，"艾克说，"我们要像泡泡糖似的黏在一起。"可紧接着鲍勃一把抱起了克鲁德，然后带着他去了隔壁的房间。"不是说好了要像泡泡糖似的黏在一起的嘛！"克鲁德大叫，"下一个就轮到你了！"艾克在屋子里走来走去、走来走去，直到……

　　一大团飘浮在半空中的白色东西突然闯进了房间里。

　　"啊！幽灵啊，我就知道他们会出现的。"艾克一边大叫一边飞快地冲向桌子底下，结果却撞到了鼻子。

　　"我的鼻子！我的鼻子！幽灵弄伤了我的鼻子！"

　　"是我啊，哥们儿。"克鲁德说。艾克盯着那一大团白色的飘浮物，这才发现他下面竟然有四条腿。

　　"脱下来！脱下来！"艾克生气地嚷嚷。

　　克鲁德晃晃悠悠地走到了大镜子跟前，对着镜子说："我觉得我可太漂亮了。"

　　"这里有一只幽灵，就会出现更多的幽灵。"艾克催促道，"快脱下来！"

"接下来到你啦。"鲍勃招手示意艾克跟着他走。"哦，不，"艾克拒绝道，"我这么小可不能当幽灵，我这么可爱更不能当幽灵了，我、我还、还是活的啊！"

艾克飞奔着冲到椅子的下面，蜷成一团，死死地抱着一条椅子腿儿："救救我吧，克鲁德，我们说好了要一起当泡泡糖的！"

　　可是鲍勃上来又拉又拽，艾克的爪子一个接一个地松开了。砰！砰！鲍勃抱起艾克便朝隔壁的房间走去。"挺住啊，哥们儿，"克鲁德说，"你可千万不要哭鼻子哟！"

　　过了几分钟，艾克慢吞吞地走了回来，他脑袋上戴了一顶巨大的晃晃悠悠的假发。"我看起来像什么啊？"艾克问。

　　"你看起来像一只贵宾犬，"克鲁德回答，"而且是一只吃了彩虹的贵宾犬。"

　　鲍勃突然把一个又大又红的东西按在了艾克的鼻子上。"喔，"克鲁德说，"我认为你现在看上去像个小丑了。"

"啊！小丑比幽灵还要可怕，快拿掉！快把它拿掉！"艾克不停地转着圈跑，上蹿下跳。当他终于停了下来时，"阿……嚏！"艾克鼻子上的东西被他喷了出去。

鲍勃重新把它捡了起来，然后更用力地按在艾克的鼻子上。

　　"阿……嚏！阿……嚏！"那东西又一次被喷了出去。"我觉得你对小丑过敏哎。"克鲁德说。

　　"我也这么觉得，"艾克说，"不过你说的过……敏是什么意思啊？"

　　"没什么。"克鲁德说。

到了晚上，克鲁德和艾克还穿着他们的节日装扮。屋外刮起了风，树上的树叶被吹得哗啦响。"我们出门去散个步吧，"鲍勃说，"就去公园转一转好了。"

"我才不要穿成这样出门呢。"克鲁德说道。

"没错，绝对不行。"艾克说道。

"就现在！"鲍勃说完给克鲁德和艾克扣上了牵引绳，牵着他们往人行道走去。

　　"快快快，"克鲁德说，"得在那个家伙发现我们之前快点过去。"他使劲儿拽着牵引绳往前走。就在这时，他们头顶上方突然出现了一个人，紧接着就听到一声刺耳的尖叫。

　　"我跟着你行动……"艾克悄声说。他们同时抬头向上看去。

马丁太太越过围栏看了过来。她头上戴着一顶黑色的女巫帽，被大风吹得都歪了。绒球小姐缠在马丁太太的脖子上，她头上戴着一顶镶嵌着金色和蓝色珠宝的王冠。"她装扮的是谁呀？"艾克问。

"别问了。"克鲁德回答。

"我是克娄巴特拉。"绒球小姐说。她像在舔皇家棒棒糖似的轮流舔着自己的两只爪子。

"克娄……谁？"艾克问道。

"埃及艳后。"绒球小姐解释，"我在尼罗河历经沉浮，整个大地都归我主宰，所有人在我面前都要鞠躬行礼。"她瞪着艾克说："现在给我鞠躬行礼！"

艾克立马低下头，可他动作有点快，重心不稳地朝着左边滚去，然后又朝右边滚去，最后滚到了克鲁德的身上。

绒球小姐发出嘶嘶的笑声，然后看向了克鲁德，说："轮到你了。"

"绝对不可能。"克鲁德说。

　　克鲁德用力地拉拽牵引绳。"快走啊，鲍勃，"他汪汪大叫，"公园应该也坏不到哪儿去了！"克鲁德和艾克拉着鲍勃向大街走去。他们绕过一个街角，再绕过一个街角，就来到了公园。门口立着一块指示牌：

汪汪游行庆典

　　然而克鲁德和艾克根本就没有注意到。

着装大比拼！

4

"看看这些孩子们啊，"艾克说，"有小吸血鬼、小公主，还有那些看起来无聊透顶的爸爸们。"

"你还记不记得去年？"克鲁德问，"就是鲍勃给我们零食的时候。"

艾克舔了舔嘴巴："记得记得，简直好吃极了。我汪汪大叫，等得口水都流下来了，然后就抢到了零食。"

"你吃了好多零食！"克鲁德说。

"吃了足足有一周呢。"艾克回忆。

"你是足足病了一周。"克鲁德说。

"美好的时光啊！"艾克感叹道。

　　鲍勃牵着他们走过人群。克鲁德摇摇晃晃地走着，艾克摇摇晃晃地跟在克鲁德的身后。鲍勃走到一个巨大的舞台前停了下来。舞台上坐着很多只狗狗，有青蛙装扮的狗狗，有恐龙装扮的狗狗，以及穿着各式各样礼服的狗狗。

　　"让我想一想啊，"艾克说，"这都是些什么啊？"

"一场恶梦。"克鲁德说。

"我是在做梦吗?"艾克问,他使劲儿眨了眨眼睛。

"没有,哥们儿,这是一场装扮比赛。"

"你的意思是说……"艾克问。

"没错,"克鲁德说,"鲍勃就是要让我们参加这个比赛,他欺骗了我们。"

　　一个穿着牛奶卡通造型的男士走上了舞台,紧接着一个穿着曲奇饼干造型的女士也走上了舞台,然后站在了男士的身旁。"欢迎参加比赛!"牛奶人说道,"请把你们的狗狗带上台来吧,裁判已经就位了。"

21

"那么我们的奖品是什么呢？"曲奇女士说，"获得掌声最响亮的狗狗就能赢得那些奖品。"她指着一座巨大的银色奖杯，里面装满了狗狗零食。

"好吧，我改变主意了。"克鲁德说。

"我都听你的。"艾克说。

"我们要赢得这场比赛。"克鲁德决定。

狗狗们一只接一只走上台去开始比赛，人群中发出一阵又一阵的笑声和掌声，而且声音越来越响亮。

"哇哦！"艾克大叫。

"我们一定会赢的。"克鲁德说。

终于轮到他们登场了。"看起来要够萌才行。"克鲁德叮嘱道。

"我不一直就是这么萌萌的嘛！"艾克说道。

克鲁德忍不住翻了个白眼儿："跟紧我！"

　　鲍勃领着他们走上舞台，开始了表演。克鲁德用后腿站立起来，然后大声地嚎叫："嗷嗷嗷！"台下观众鼓起了掌。紧接着艾克也用后腿站立起来，可他重心不稳，一头栽倒在地，台下观众一边大笑一边鼓起了掌。可惜，这掌声还不够响亮。

　　"我们还得再加把劲儿啊！"克鲁德说。

　　"可是我们还能做些什么呢？"艾克问道。

　　"试一试空翻。"克鲁德说。

　　艾克一扭一扭地走到舞台边上，他先是助跑了一小段，然后起跳，紧接着开始了一个接一个的空翻。台下观众的掌声更大了，但还是不够。

"继续翻啊！"克鲁德大叫道。艾克摇着尾巴，又开始助跑。

空翻 旋转 撞击

艾克叽里咕噜地撞上了克鲁德，克鲁德又叽里咕噜地撞到了鲍勃，鲍勃撞翻了银色的奖杯，奖杯里的狗狗零食全都撒在了他们身上。裁判看上去非常生气，但是观众却欢呼了起来。

最棒狗狗

艾克从糖果堆里探出头来："嘎吱嘎吱！我们得到了最多的掌声呢！"

"是的，我们是最多的，"克鲁德说，"我们这就回家去吧，得赶快把这身装扮脱下来。"

"快点吧，鲍勃！"他们汪汪大叫着，"别忘了把我们赢的狗狗零食带上。这真是有史以来最棒的一个节日！"

英文原文

Meet the Characters

Ick

Crud

Miss Puffy

Bob

Mrs. Martin

It's Halloween!

"Boo!" yelled Crud.

"Ruff! Woof! Ruff! You scared the doggie bones out of me," said Ick.

"It's that time of year," said Crud.

"You mean pumpkins with bad teeth? Witches? And kids dressed as ghosts?"

"Yes," said Crud. "It's Halloween."

过节啦！

"嘣！"克鲁德突然大叫一声。

"哇！啊！哇！你吓得我差点灵魂出窍了！"艾克大叫。

"已经到了每年的那个时候啦！"克鲁德说。

"你是说坏牙的南瓜、女巫，还有装扮成幽灵的孩子们，是吗？"艾克问。

"是的！"克鲁德兴奋地说，"要过节啦！"

1

2

"哦吼。"艾克说。

"今年想都别想,"克鲁德说,"他休想再把我打扮成一根热狗了。"

"你这已经算是不错了,"艾克抱怨道,"鲍勃去年把我放到婴儿车里,我还要拿着婴儿摇铃。孩子们看到我的样子时,吓得尖叫着就晕倒了。"

"好吧,所以今年我们一定不能再让事情重演了。"克鲁德说道,"跟紧我。"

"我已经像泡泡糖似的黏着你了。"艾克说。

3

艾克吓得浑身发抖:"这个时候会有很多很多的幽灵,我害怕幽灵,而且他们住在阁楼里,他们还会吃小狗狗。"

"我会保护你的,哥们儿。"克鲁德说。

这时,鲍勃抱着两个盒子走了进来,每个盒子上面都写着:"狗狗服装"。

Ick shivered. "Halloween has too many ghosts. I don't like ghosts. They live in attics. And they eat little dogs."

"I'll protect you, buddy," said Crud.

Just then Bob walked in holding two boxes. On each was written: *Dog Costume.*

"Uh-oh," said Ick.

"Not this year," said Crud. "I'm not letting him dress me up like a hot dog again."

"You had it easy," moaned Ick. "Bob put me in a buggy last year. I had a baby rattle! Kids screamed and fainted when they saw me."

"Well, this year will be different," said Crud. "Stick with me."

"Like bubblegum," said Ick.

I Look Boo-tiful

"Come, Crud," called Bob. Crud acted like he didn't hear. "Crud!" yelled Bob again. "Come!"

"Not gonna do it," whispered Crud.

"Me neither," said Ick. "We're stuck together like bubblegum." Just then Bob scooped up Crud. And took him into the next room. "Nice sticking like bubblegum," yelled Crud. "You're next." Ick paced back and forth. And forth and back. Until a big white blob floated into the room.

"AAOOOHH! A ghost! I knew it!" yelled Ick. He dashed under a table. And used his nose to stop.

"AAAGGGHH!" yelled Ick. "My nose. My nose! A ghost broke my nose."

我看上去可太漂亮啦！

"快过来呀，克鲁德！"鲍勃叫道。克鲁德就像没听见似的。"克鲁德，"鲍勃又叫道，"快过来呀！"

"我才不去呢，"克鲁德小声嘀咕。

"我也不去，"艾克说，"我们就像泡泡糖似的粘在一起。"可紧接着鲍勃一把抱起了克鲁德，然后带着他去了隔壁的房间。"不是说好了要像泡泡糖似的粘在一起的嘛！"克鲁德大叫，"下一个就轮到你了！"艾克在屋子里走来走去，走来走去，直到……

一大团飘浮在半空中的白色东西突然闯进了房间里。

"啊！幽灵啊，我就知道他们会出现的。"艾克一边大叫一边飞快地冲向桌子底下，结果却撞到了鼻子。

"我的鼻子！我的鼻子！幽灵弄伤了我的鼻子！"

4

5

"It's me, buddy," said Crud. Ick stared at the white blob. It had four fat paws under it.

"Take it off! Take it off!" yelled Ick.

Crud waddled to the big mirror. "I think I look boo-tiful."

"Where there's one ghost, there's more," said Ick. "Take it off!"

"You're next," said Bob. He waved for Ick to follow him. "Oh, no," said Ick. "I'm too young to be a ghost. I'm too cute to be a ghost. I'm too…too…alive."

Ick darted under a chair. He slid on his belly. Then he grabbed onto the chair leg. "Save me, Crud! Be like bubblegum!"

可是鲍勃上来又拉又拽，艾克的爪子一个接一个地松开了。砰！砰！鲍勃抱起艾克便朝隔壁的房间走去。"挺住啊，哥们儿，"克鲁德说，"你可千万不要哭鼻子哟！"

过了几分钟，艾克慢吞吞地走了回来，他脑袋上戴了一项巨大的晃晃悠悠的假发。"我看起来像什么啊？"艾克问。

"你看起来像一只贵宾犬，"克鲁德回答，"而且是一只吃了彩虹的贵宾犬。"

鲍勃突然把一个又大又红的东西按在了艾克的鼻子上。"噫，"克鲁德说，"我认为你现在看上去像个小丑了。"

8

9

Bob pulled and tugged. Ick's paws slipped off one by one. Pop! Pop! Bob scooped him up and carried Ick into the next room. "Hang in there, Buddy," said Crud. "No need to boo-hoo about it."

In a few minutes, Ick crawled back. A big wig wiggled on his head. "What am I?" he asked.

"You look like a poodle," said Crud. "A poodle who ate a rainbow."

Bob plopped something big and red on Ick's nose. "Oh," said Crud. "I think you're a clown."

"AAAGGGHH! Clowns are scarier than ghosts. Take it off. Take it off!" Ick spun in a circle. He flipped. He flopped. And when he stopped…"Ahhh-choo!" The nose shot off.

Bob grabbed it. He stuck the nose on Ick a bit tighter.

"Ahhh-choo. Ahhh-choo." The nose shot off again. "I think you're allergic to clowns," said Crud.

"I think so, too," said Ick. "What does ah-ler-jik mean?"

"Never mind," said Crud.

3

Meeting Cleopatra

By evening, Ick and Crud still had their costumes on. Outside the wind whipped the leaves up and down. And around and around. "Time for a quick walk," said Bob. "Let's go to the park."

"Not dressed like this," said Crud.

"No way," said Ick.

"Now!" said Bob. He snapped on Crud and Ick's leashes. And plopped the two down on the sidewalk.

"Hurry," said Crud. "Before you-know-who sees us." He tugged on the leash. Just then something moved above them. It let out a piggy squeal.

"I will if you will," whispered Ick. Crud and Ick looked up.

37

马丁太太越过围栏看了过来。她头上戴着一顶黑色的女巫帽，被大风吹得都歪了。绒球小姐缠在马丁太太的脖子上，她头上戴着一顶镶着金色和蓝色珠宝的王冠。"她装扮的是谁呀？"艾克问。

"别问了。"克鲁德回答。

"我是克娄巴特拉。"绒球小姐说。她像在舔皇家棒棒糖似的轮流舔着自己的两只爪子。

"克娄……谁？"艾克问道。

"埃及艳后。"绒球小姐解释，"我在尼罗河历经沉浮，整个大地都归我主宰，所有人在我面前都要鞠躬行礼。"她瞪着艾克说："现在给我鞠躬行礼！"

14   15

Mrs. Martin peeked over the fence. Her black witch's hat bent in the wind. Miss Puffy curled around her neck. She wore a crown with blue and gold jewels. "Who is she supposed to be?" said Ick.

"Don't ask," said Crud.

"I am Cleopatra," said Miss Puffy. She licked her paws like royal lollipops.

"Cleo-who?" asked Ick.

"The queen of Egypt," said Miss Puffy. "I float up and down the Nile River. I rule all the land. Everyone must bow down to me." She stared at Ick. "Bow now!"

艾克立马低下头，可他动作有点快，重心不稳地朝着左边滚去，然后又朝右边滚去，最后滚到了克鲁德的身上。

绒球小姐发出嘶嘶的笑声，然后看向了克鲁德，说："轮到你了。"

"绝对不可能。"克鲁德说。

克鲁德用力地拉拽牵引绳。"快走啊，鲍勃，"他汪汪大叫，"公园应该也坏不到哪儿去了！"克鲁德和艾克拉着鲍勃向大街走去。他们绕过一个街角，再绕过一个街角，就来到了公园。门口立着一块指示牌：

汪汪游行庆典

然而克鲁德和艾克根本就没有注意到。

16

17

Ick dipped his head. But a little too fast. He rolled to the left. Then to the right. And rolled right into Crud.

Miss Puffy hissed a laugh. "Your turn," she said. And looked at Crud.

"Not gonna happen," said Crud.

He tugged on the leash. "Come on, Bob," he barked. "The park can't be worse." Crud and Ick pulled Bob down the street. Around the corner. Around another corner. And into the park. A new sign hung on the entrance.

BIG BARKIN' HALLOWEEN PARADE

But Ick and Crud didn't see it.

Costume Contest

"Look at all the kids," said Ick. "Tiny vampires. Mini princesses. And dads who look bored."

"Remember last year?" asked Crud. "When Bob gave out treats."

Ick licked his lips. "Yes and yum. I'd bark, wait for the drop, then grab the treats."

"You ate a lot!" said Crud.

"Enough for a week," said Ick.

"You were sick for a week," said Crud.

"Good times," said Ick.

Bob led them through the crowd. Crud wiggled and wagged. Ick wagged and wiggled behind him. Bob stopped at a big stage. On it sat dogs. Frog dogs.

一个穿着牛奶卡通造型的男士走上了舞台，紧接着一个穿着曲奇饼干造型的女士也走上了舞台，然后站在了男士的身旁。"欢迎参加比赛！"牛奶人说道，"请把你们的狗狗带上台来吧，裁判已经就位了。"

Dinosaur dogs. And dogs in dresses.

"Hold the doggie door," said Ick. "What is this?"

"A bad dream," said Crud.

"Am I dreaming?" asked Ick. He blinked his eyes really hard.

"No, buddy. This is a costume contest."

"You don't think…?" asked Ick.

"Yes," said Crud. "Bob is entering us in the contest. He tricked us!"

A man dressed as a milk carton came on stage. A woman dressed as a cookie stood beside him. "Welcome," said the milk man. "Bring your dogs to the stage. The judges are ready."

"And what do you win?" asked the woman. "The dog with the loudest claps gets all of this!" She pointed to a large silver cup. It was filled with doggie treats.

"Well, this changes things," said Crud.

"I will if you will," said Ick.

"We got this," said Crud.

Dog after dog walked across the stage. The crowd laughed. The crowd clapped. Louder and louder.

"Uh-oh," said Ick.

"We got this," said Crud.

Then it was their turn. "Just look cute," said Crud.

"That's how I always look," said Ick.

Crud rolled his eyes. "Follow me."

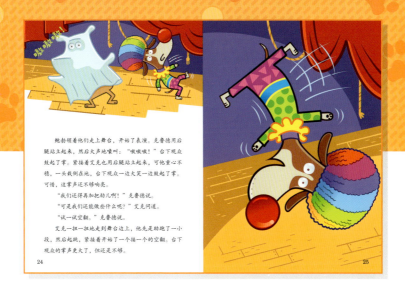

鲍勃领着他们走上舞台，开始了表演。克鲁德用后腿站立起来，然后大声地嗥叫："嗷嗷嗷！"台下观众鼓起了掌。紧接着艾克也用后腿站立起来，可他重心不稳，一头栽倒在地，台下观众一边大笑一边鼓起了掌。可惜，这掌声还不够响亮。

"我们还得再加把劲儿啊！"克鲁德说。

"可是我们还能做些什么呢？"艾克问道。

"试一试空翻。"克鲁德说。

艾克一扭一扭地走到舞台边上，他先是助跑了一小段，然后起跳，紧接着开始了一个接一个的空翻。台下观众的掌声更大了，但还是不够。

Bob led them on stage. Crud stood on his hind legs. He howled "AHHOOH!" The crowd clapped. Ick stood on his hind legs. He tipped over. The crowd laughed and clapped. But not loud enough.

"We need to do something more," said Crud.

"What?" asked Ick.

"Try your flip," said Crud.

Ick wiggled to the side of the stage. He took a little run. Then he flipped and flipped. The crowd clapped louder. But not loud enough.

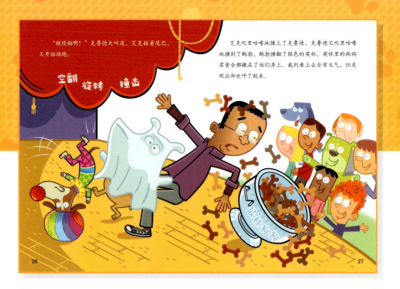

"Do it again," yelled Crud. Ick wagged his tail. Then he took another run.

Ick rolled into Crud. Crud rolled into Bob. Bob rolled into the big bowl. And the doggie treats spilled on top of them all. The judges looked mad. But the crowd went wild.

艾克从糖果堆里探出头来："嘎吱嘎吱！我们得到了最多的掌声呢！"

"是的，我们是最多的，"克鲁德说，"我们这就回家去吧，得赶快把这身装扮脱下来。"

"快点吧，鲍勃！"他们汪汪大叫着，"别忘了把我们赢的狗狗零食带上。这真是有史以来最棒的一个节日！"

28

Ick poked his head out of the mess. "Crunch! Crunch! We got the most claps," he said.

"Yes, we did," said Crud. "Let's go home. And get out of these costumes."

"Come on Bob," they barked. "And don't forget the doggie treats. It's going to be a happy, happy Halloween after all!"